reading in multilingual classrooms

Viv Edwards

Reading and Language Information Centre
University of Reading

For Frank Rees, story reader extraordinary

Acknowledgments
Grateful thanks to to Angela Redfern, Prue Goodwin and Chris Routh for reading and commenting on various drafts; to the staff, children and parents of Redlands Primary School and Prospect School Reading for allowing us to take photographs; and to Frank Monaghan for suggestions on resources.

Meeting the needs of bilingual pupils
This book is part of a series of training materials which consists of three separate packs:
- *Reading in multilingual classrooms*
- *Writing in multilingual classrooms*
- *Speaking and listening in multilingual classrooms*

Each pack comprises:
- a course leader's handbook
- overhead transparencies
- handouts
- a teacher's book

The teacher's books are also available separately.

Publications of related interest
Other titles from the Reading and Language Information Centre of interest to teachers in multilingual classrooms include:

Building bridges: multilingual resources for children
Multilingual Resources for Children Project

The AIMER Year Book

Annually updated lists of anti-racist, multicultural teaching materials to support all areas of the curriculum, as well as community language teaching and language support teaching.

The multicultural guide to children's literature 0-12
Edited by Rosemary Stones

Working with parents
Penny Kenway

ISBN 0 7049 0769 0

Reading and Language Information Centre
University of Reading
Bulmershe Court
Earley
Reading RG6 1HY

Contents

Introduction

Multilingual classrooms are complex communities. Children come from many different language backgrounds; they also have varying levels of experience with the written word. Very young and recently arrived children may not be able to read at all. Some older children read fluently in two and – in some cases – three different languages. Others read only in English or in the community language.

Teachers' experience also varies. Those who work with younger children may feel confident about the methods which they use with native English speakers, but unsure as to how they should approach second language learners. Those who work with older children may have received little or no training in the teaching of reading.

This book explores the many dimensions of reading in multilingual classrooms. In particular, it focuses on:

- the process of learning to read
- reading behaviours of second language learners
- the different approaches to the teaching of reading
- practical ways to support bilingual readers
- resources for reading in English and in community languages
- the assessment of children's development as readers.

The reading process

It used to be thought that the reader's task was to decode the written word. This assumption was first challenged when researchers began analyzing the strategies of fluent readers. When you consider that it can take up to four times as long to read a passage aloud as it does to read it silently, it is obvious that something far more complex than word by word decoding is taking place. It seems that the eye picks out key pieces of information and that the brain fills in the rest.

The analysis of the mistakes or 'miscues' which children make when reading aloud offer us a 'window' on the reading process: they show us how we use our knowledge of language, life and how stories work to predict what lies ahead. As we proceed, our predictions are confirmed or modified in what is sometimes called a psycholinguistic guessing game.

There are three main categories of miscue:

- *Grapho-phonic miscues* require a knowledge of the sound system and the way that sounds are represented in writing. They happen when the reader replaces the word in the text with one that sounds or looks like it but has a different meaning, eg *food* for *foot.*
- *Syntactic miscues* draw on knowledge of the grammatical structure of the language and take several forms:
  - – they can fit the overall syntax (eg *a sensible idea* for *a stupid idea*)
  - – they can reorder the text without changing the meaning (eg *he called the list of names out* for *he called out the list of names*)
  - – they can reflect the way the reader speaks (eg *I done it, he come here*).
- *Semantic miscues* draw on the readers knowledge of meaning. They are closely related to the actual word in the text, eg *he handed her a plate of* ***biscuits*** for *he handed her a plate of* ***cakes.***

Textual cohesion

Knowledge of the language is essential if we are to predict what comes next. But successful readers also need to know how texts work. In more extended writing, sentences relate to each in a variety of ways. To carry an idea through a text, readers need to be able to understand the cohesive links between sentences.

In this text:

- *It* refers back to *Reading*
- *Reading, Thames Valley, south-east England, towns* and *site* are all related words; so, too, are *museum, excavated, Roman, artefacts* and *centuries*
- *Thus* links the last sentence with the previous one

Reading lies in the heart of the Thames Valley. It is typical of many other towns in south-east England. The museum includes excavated Roman artefacts. Thus we know the site has been occupied for many centuries

(conclusion)

Bilingual readers

For a considerable period of time, it was believed that children learning English needed a sound foundation in the spoken language before they were introduced to the written word. More recently it has been possible to demonstrate that even children who speak virtually no English – and who have no previous experience of reading – recognize print in the environment: *MacDonalds, Hospital, Stop* and so on.

The position of children already literate in a community language is rather different. There is evidence that existing skills are readily transferred to English. Reading also has certain advantages for children who feel shy or inhibited. When encountering an unknown word or expression, they may feel more comfortable rereading the word in context than asking someone to repeat what they have said.

It is also important to remember that reading comprehension often outstrips competence in speaking. Bilingual children sometimes read in a monotone which suggests they haven't understood. When they are questioned about what they have read, they may not be able to answer. Yet when the same questions are put in the community language, it often becomes clear that they have deduced the meaning from the context or the illustrations.

Whatever their prior experience of the written word, reading helps children to learn the language: the more widely they read, the more exposure they will have to key vocabulary and structures.

Typical reading behaviours

Bilingual readers can't use the structures and meanings of texts to predict as effectively as native speakers. They may also be unfamiliar with the cultural content of their reading. Many stories contain references to unfamiliar objects or events. And details about everyday experiences are often omitted because the writer assumes readers will be able to supply their own 'scripts' or understandings of what is taking place. However, scripts can differ from one culture to another. Take the following sentence from a book called *Auntie Pat in hospital* (cited in Wallace 1985):

> Sally's daddy said: we are going to see Auntie Pat in hospital. Sally and her daddy went to a shop to get some ...

'Flowers' may not be so easily predictable by Asian children, if buying flowers is not a part of their expectations when visiting people in hospital.

While there is, of course, enormous variation, certain kinds of reading behaviour are very characteristic of second language learners. Teachers often notice:

- a higher proportion of grapho-phonic miscues and substitutions that change the meaning of the text
- 'mechanical' reading: a low number of errors and a tendency to hypercorrect.

Different experiences of reading

... One day Gurdeep's mother showed me all the family's holy books. Before she opened the cabinet where they are kept we washed our hands and Gurdeep's sister chose to cover her head and wash her mouth. Gurdeep's mother reached to the back of the shelves and carefully drew out prayer books and stories of the lives of the Gurus, each covered with a gold and purple cloth. Then she showed me a volume of the Guru Granth Sahib and unwrapped the fold of cloth to reveal a large and beautifully bound book ...

Minns (1990)

One of the most common myths about literacy in minority communities is that children have very limited exposure to books and their parents have little interest in reading. In fact, all the evidence suggests this is not true. Minority communities place a very high value on literacy, particularly when there is a link between language and religion. Like Christians, Jews, Moslems and Sikhs attach enormous importance to holy texts.

The findings of a recent research project on the the Bangladeshi community in East London (Gregory 1993a), for instance, underline the importance of literacy in minority communities. The area in question has several shops which sell the Qur'ān and poetry books, autobiographies, newspapers and children's books in Bengali. Most grocery shops also sell children's primers for learning to read Bengali. These books are displayed in a bookcase in the homes of many of the children in the study while reading primers, exercise books, pencils and often a special school bag are kept away from younger children, usually out of sight in a high cupboard.

Some children in the study received one to one tuition in Bengali; others attended classes in private homes or community centres. Most went to Bengali classes between 5pm and 7pm three times a week; they spent a similar amount of time in mosque classes learning to read Classical Arabic. In all cases, parents who often have very limited means are making a financial investment in their children's education. The notion that literacy is not valued, or that children have only limited exposure to the written word clearly has no foundation.

Community language teaching is not, of course, limited to the Bangladeshi community. As early as 1985, the Linguistic Minorities Project reported that classes in 18 different languages were being offered to over 8,500 children in just three English local education authorities. The same interest in language maintenance can be seen in other countries, too. According to the Canadian Ethnocultural Council (1988), 72 school boards in Ontario were offering 4,364 classes in 58 different languages to over 90,000 students. And Horvath & Vaughan (1991) document some 58 community languages currently being taught in Australia.

Children thus have very varied experiences with print which, inevitably, have an impact on their attitudes towards reading in the classroom. By looking at a range of literacy practices, it is possible to identify potential areas of misunderstanding between home and school and to think of ways of working together more closely to develop children's reading.

The Black experience of literacy

For a long time, it was believed that learning to read was simply a matter of acquiring certain skills. More recently, we have started to understand the social dimension of literacy learning. The work of Shirley Brice Heath (1983) has been particularly influential. In the Black community of Trackton in South Carolina, for instance, children have no books. Emphasis is put on reading to learn rather than learning to read. Encounters with print tend to be functional: picking out the relevant parts of instruction booklets so that you can assemble or modify a piece of equipment, or reading the price tags in the local store to know that you are making a good buy.

In Trackton, anyone who chooses to read alone is dismissed as lacking social skills: reading is considered a social activity. The evening newspaper is usually read aloud on the front porch, starting with the obituaries and followed by the job vacancies, advertisements for sales and captions beneath pictures and headlines. Circulars and other letters of general interest are also read aloud. All generate a great deal of discussion. Shirley Brice Heath(1983: 200–1) talks of the

> repeated metaphors, comparisons and fast-paced, overlapping language as Trackton residents move from print to what it means in their lives. On some occasions, they attend to the text itself; on others, they use it only as a starting point for wide-ranging talk. On all occasions, they bring in knowledge related to the text and interpret beyond the text for their own context; in so doing, they achieve a new synthesis of information from the text and the joint experience of community members.

Maktab literacy

Many Moslem children, too, will have experienced very different ways of interacting with the printed word. In traditional Moslem religious schools or 'maktabs', children learn, among other things, to recite by heart whole passages of the Qur'ān. Maktabs have definite boundaries between 'work' and 'play' which make them very different from mainstream school.

The same principles often spill over from Qur'ānic to voluntary community language classes including Urdu, Bengali and Gujarati. Children questioned in the study by Gregory (1993a), for instance, were clear that they 'read and write' in Bengali school and 'play' in English school. In classes which often last for two hours without a break, children remain seated on the floor or at the table and all talk is directed to the task in hand. Tuition is exact and direct. The child answers and will be told either, 'Yes' or 'Not like that, like this.'

The skills which children need for reading the Qur'ān are very different from those required in school. Brian Street (1984), for instance, argues that maktab literacy often produces children who recognize passages they have memorized by their position on the page, layout and style rather than by 'cracking the phonemic code'.

Yet despite the differences between maktab and school literacy, Moslem children acquire many skills in mosque classes which can be easily transferred to reading in English. They understand the concept of 'word', directionality and different ways of breaking up the page. Maktab literacy also helps develop skills for non-sequential reading. In order to find specific passages to justify an argument, students learn to thumb their way around the Qur'ān and other texts using, for example, headings and contents pages.

The Chinese experience of literacy

The Chinese experience of literacy has much in common with maktab literacy. Great importance is attached to the values of Confucianism which include respect for parents and achievement in education. There is a strict division between work and play. Children sit in rows and do as the teacher directs them. They practise ideographs over and over until they are perfect. If they forget or misplace a single stroke, they may completely change the meaning of the character, so close attention to detail is essential. Like in the maktab, children who attend Chinese community classes recite words in chorus after the teacher. They learn through repetition, memorization and careful copying.

Books are held in very high esteem but parents believe that children must prove themselves worthy through hard work. In much the same way that Moslem children are given the Qur'ān when they have worked their way through Arabic primers, many Chinese children are rewarded with books only when they have learned to read.

These expectations have serious implications for children who experience a very different approach to literacy in mainstream schooling. Gregory (1993b), for instance, describes the enthusiasm of Tony and his family from Hong Kong when he starts school. Within a few months, however, Tony has started to reject his teacher's attempts to help him. He is focusing on individual words and is more interested in labelling people and things in the illustrations than in trying to predict what comes next.

When the class teacher talks with Tony's family, she begins to understand the problem. Tony's grandfather is upset about what he feels are the very low expectations of the school. He shows her a drawing which has been labelled 'ToNy' and expresses exasperation that his grandson cannot even write his name correctly.

Caught between the different approaches of his Chinese and British schools – Tony seems to 'switch off'. The root of the problem, however, would seem to lie not so much in the differences between the two systems as in the fact that Tony's family assumes that the same principles should operate in both systems. This confusion is exacerbated by the fact that Tony's teachers have not explained precisely what they are trying to achieve. Children from 'non-mainstream' families need to relate their own experiences of literacy to those of the school. The mainstream teacher has a vital role to play in this process.

Implications for teachers

Children from White middle class homes will be familiar with classroom literacy practices. Children from minority cultures, however, have to negotiate a complex course between very different approaches to the written word. These differences have important implications both for teachers' relationships with parents and for the kind of information which they need to share.

The role of parents

Traditionally, parents were seen as having little or no part to play in the formal education of their children. More recently, parents who fail to provide the same kinds of literacy experience as the school have been blamed for their children's underachievement. This response is overly simplistic. We need to draw on parents' knowledge and experience to transform what is offered in school, rather than trying to transfer school practices to the home.

While our understanding of how this can be achieved is imprecise, there can be little doubt as to the value of parental involvement. Tizard, Schofield, Hewison (1982), for instance, point to the role which parents play in listening to their children reading. Children chosen at random from two inner city schools in the London borough of Haringey were given books to read to their parents at home. This extra practice produced

highly significant improvements, even when their parents couldn't speak English.

Home-school notebooks are an important part of many schemes for involving parents in their children's reading. One such initiative is reported by Penny Kenway (1994) in her work at Wellington Primary School in west London. In a meeting to introduce the scheme to parents, discussion focussed on ways of supporting children's reading development and the educational reasons for involving parents.

Parental anxiety about what to write in the home-school notebook was also addressed. A mock-up of a notebook was pinned on a large board. Comments ranged from the very simple 'Jerome liked the story, especially the part about the cat' to more complex descriptions: 'Joe wanted to know why Sally was crying. He said this book was beautiful and now knows why she was crying.' It was also explained that parents were welcome to make comments in community languages which would be translated by bilingual support staff. The response was enthusiastic. Parents and children clearly enjoyed sharing the books and felt more confident about writing in the notebook in both English and community languages.

Making expectations explicit

The knowledge that the school's interpretation of reading is only one among many carries heavy responsibilities for the teacher. When children start school, they bring with them a picture of themselves as learners, based on all that has happened up to this point. Teachers need to find ways to acknowledge this pre-school experience. In order to do this, they need to create opportunities for discussing previous activities with children, their parents and others with the same background as the children.

A useful framework for this kind of discussion is the *Primary language record* (Barrs *et al* 1988) which records children's language experience from the perspective of teachers, parents and children themselves. It is helpful for the teacher to know, for example, if the child is familiar with scripts which run from right to left, or left to right; whether the script hangs down from or rests on a real or imaginary line; or whether they are currently learning to read and write the home language in community classes. By consulting children and parents, teachers not only gather useful information; they also show that they appreciate the knowledge which children bring with them to school.

If parents and teachers are to work together, teachers must also find ways of making explicit the school's view of what counts as reading. The practices which have evolved over the last thirty years and which reflect our greater understanding of the reading process are not always clear to White middle class parents. Eve Gregory's case study of the family from Hong Kong leaves no doubt that parents who have grown up in different traditions find these practices even more confusing.

The teaching of reading

Very few schools rely exclusively on one method of teaching reading. Most teachers use a judicious mix, wherever possible matching different methods to the needs of individual children. The presence of bilingual children in the class, however, sometimes raises questions as to whether this judicious mix is appropriate. When a child's English is heavily accented, for instance, many teachers wonder if a stronger emphasis on phonics might be helpful. Against this background, it is useful to look at the various approaches to the teaching of reading from the perspective of bilingual children.

The skills approach

Traditionally, learning to read was seen in terms of developing a set of skills which would allow you to decode the written word. 'Phonics' and 'Look and say' are both examples of the skills approach.

Phonics

Phonics teaching draws attention to sounds and their relationship with letters. The assumption that letters, or combinations of letters, represent sounds is reasonable in phonemically regular writing systems like Spanish. However, the relationship between sounds and letters in English is rather more complex. The 26 letters of the English alphabet are used to represent approximately 44 distinctive sounds or phonemes. Sometimes, as in *rough, though, thought, bough,* individual letters represent a number of different sounds. At other times (eg *knight, psalm*), they are not pronounced at all.

a

sound	listen	say
ra	rat	rat
pa	pat	pat
sa	sat	sat
ga	gap	gap
la	lap	lap
ta	tap	tap
ba	bag	bag

Phonics stresses letter sound relationships

Overreliance on Phonics has been criticized for other reasons, too. For instance, children's ability to distinguish between sounds develops at different rates, with boys typically experiencing greater difficulty than girls. Children with auditory problems such as glue ear will also find it difficult to learn to read when there is a heavy emphasis on Phonics.

Phonics teaching raises problems, too, for children learning English. At a given point in their development, they may not, for instance, be able to distinguish between pairs of English sounds such as *s* and *sh* (*shin* and *sin*), *r* and *l* (*rack* and *lack*) or *i* and *ee* (*dip* and *deep*). The teacher's instinct may well be to draw children's attention to the differences, but this may be counterproductive. Children who don't make the distinctions in their speech will be very unlikely to hear them when the teacher tries to drill them.

Just as important, children's understanding of what they read does not depend on accurate pronunciation. Scottish children, for instance, distinguish between *wh* and *w* (as in *wear* and *where*). Although English children pronounce both these sounds as *w*, they understand the meaning from the context.

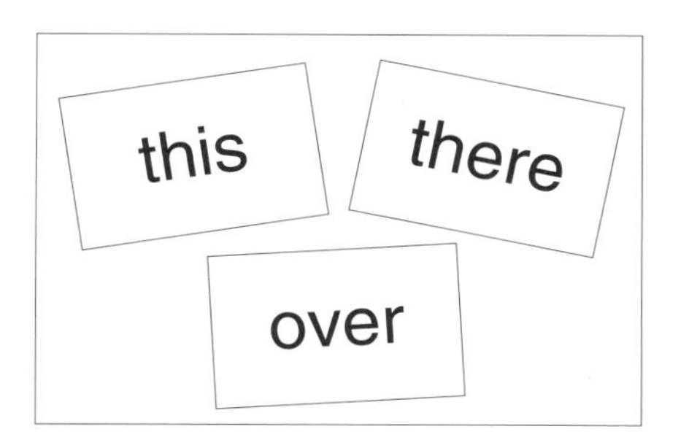

Flashcards help some but not all children

Look and say

Whereas Phonics focuses on the relationship between letters and sounds, Look and say concentrates on the relationship between words and sounds. It aims to develop the ability to name whole words, first in isolation, then in context.

Like Phonics, Look and say has been criticized on various fronts. The heavy emphasis on word recognition poses problems, for instance, for children with a poor visual memory. A more general concern is that Look and say fails to provide strategies which help children read words they haven't met before.

The skills approach: problems for bilingual readers

Look and say also has other problems which it shares with Phonics. Books written to support a skills approach tend to have a limited number of words, sound very contrived and encourage a mechanistic view of reading. In contrast, books with clear, predictable texts are easier to read and allow children to extend their experience of English structures and vocabulary.

Another problem relates to the fact that books based on a skills approach often use high frequency words with several different meanings. A child reading *Put the sock on your* – won't have any difficulty supplying *foot.* But the same child may not be able to read *foot* in *They arrived at the – of the hill.* This poses particular problems for second language learners who won't have encountered as wide a range of meanings as native speakers.

Teaching skills to best effect

It simply isn't possible to identify specific skills that can be built up in any kind of hierarchical way. Nor has it been possible to demonstrate a correlation between effective reading and performance in different subskills.This doesn't mean, of course, that teachers should ignore either the relationships between sounds and letters, or word recognition skills.

Most recent research suggests that systematic Phonics teaching is more effective when children's reading begins to take off. Before we learn to read, we hear language as a string of sounds, rather than the words we use in writing. Various activities help children relate speech to print: games such as 'I spy' which focus on initial letters; clapping and tapping to syllabic rhymes; identifying word endings (or 'rimes') in poetry and rhymes. Activities of this kind are essential for the reading development of *all* children, but are particularly important for children learning to speak English who have had less exposure to the sounds and rhythms of their second language .

Similarly, it is important for children to be able to recognize words. Reading can't take off at all without a small initial sight vocabulary and, the larger this vocabulary, the easier children will find it to read. The inevitable conclusion, though, is that teachers should not put all their trust in either Phonics or Look and say as the sole approach to the teaching of reading.

The strategies approach

The skills approach looks on the job of the reader as the decoding of the written word. From the 1960s onwards, researchers began to look more closely at the reading behaviours of fluent readers. It became clear that the aim of reading was not to decode the written word but to make meaning of the text, and that the teacher's job was to equip children with strategies which would help them to do this. The strategies approach is based on this new understanding of what happens when we read. The two main examples are the 'Apprenticeship method' and 'Language experience.'

The Apprenticeship method

We are surrounded by print: street signs, cards, letters, junk mail, calendars. By the time most children come to school they have already realized that marks on paper are a way of communicating messages.

The Apprenticeship method builds on children's prior knowledge of language, life and stories. The emphasis is on enjoying books, responding to the story and comparing it with their own experience. Children regularly read a book alongside the teacher until they feel ready to take over on their own.

Some people accuse teachers who use the Apprenticeship method of offering children no structure. In fact, schools that use this approach usually have a well planned programme for teaching the full range of strategies that children need to become fluent readers (see pages 12–15 for further discussion).

This approach can also be used with groups of children or even the whole class. Using 'Big books' – poster-sized books with large print – the teacher reads the story first, employing the same strategies for drawing children's attention to the print as in other read aloud activities; then the children join in. They learn not only from the adult model but also from their own participation and from each other. This kind of reading is free from any sense of competition or pressure.

Language experience

In a Language experience approach, children's own writing becomes their reading material. This process helps children to see the links between talking, reading and writing. They are highly motivated because the story is their own. This helps them to remember the words and ensures that their early attempts at reading are successful. Meaning is emphasized from the start.

The most widely used commercial example of Language experience is Longman's *Breakthrough to literacy*. Children compose their story by placing words printed on cards in a plastic stand and then copy the story into their books. *Breakthrough* is sometimes criticized because it is so 'fiddly': it certainly demands very good organisational skills. Some children find it difficult to manipulate the tiny word cards. They can also find it tedious to copy out their story after they have composed it in the stand. Many teachers have adapted this approach, retaining only the features which they find most useful.

But in spite of these problems, *Breakthrough* has many strengths. It also has some distinct advantages for bilingual learners. In the early stages, the teacher works with small groups of children. Bilingual children listen to the teacher and the other children as they 'rehearse' their stories. The teacher draws on everybody's contributions to make a group story. Activities of this kind provide important 'scaffolding' for children learning English.

Other features of *Breakthrough* support children's learning of English, too. The emphasis on making sentences draws children's attention to key features of English grammar such as word order. And the use of separate cards for suffixes such as *s, ing, ed* draws children's attention to grammatical devices for word building.

Some teachers are very worried about the idea of basing children's reading on their writing, because very often the stories which they dictate contain mistakes. It is important to remember that language acquisition is a developmental process. The child who dictates *Mummy goed shopping,* and has not yet realised that some past tenses are formed by changing the vowel, will continue to say *goed* in spite of the teacher's insistence on *went*. The most realistic option is for teachers to provide an accurate model in their oral and written responses, eg *Yes, I went to the shops yesterday, too.*

Breakthrough to Literacy, a commercial example of the Language experience approach

Supporting bilingual readers

Lesson Four, Thursday afternoon and 5.2 enter their English classroom to the all familiar sound of the teacher announcing the chapter to be read that day. After the class has settled down, the teacher asks the usual questions about what has been happening in the story, and, having elicited a half-hearted response, begins to read the next chapter. Five minutes later he notices that one boy, a beginner bilingual learner, is not paying attention. He stops what he is doing, goes over to the boy, points to the appropriate point in the story and then continues to read.

Fifteen minutes more pass; the teacher is still reading, the boy is not paying attention. After several more attempts to get the boy to look at the book – even though they both know he cannot read it – the teacher decides to ignore him so as to maintain the concentration of the rest of the class. A victim of a utilitarian logic of which he is blissfully unaware, the boy continues to stare out of the window. He leaves at 3.35 having gained nothing from the lesson.

Jim Lamey (1989)

Whether dealing with older children, as in the extract above, or with young children, the teacher's main concern is not just to keep them occupied, but to help them develop as readers. A whole range of strategies can be used to support reading development. They are very helpful for all children, but are particularly important when working with bilingual children.

Before you start reading

Fluent readers are very good at predicting what comes next. This is more difficult for bilingual readers who may not have the knowledge of vocabulary or grammar or the cultural content of the story to help them guess what lies ahead. So it's particularly important to help language learners develop effective strategies for prediction.

When a child chooses a book, it's important to identify key words, idioms and structures, or any aspects of the story that may seem strange for a reader from another culture. Talking about the title and the jacket, and helping the children to tell the story from the illustrations are also important preliminaries. This 'rehearsal' will help to familiarize them with vocabulary and structures they will meet in the story.

Familiarity with the story is essential if children are going to make good predictions. You can help by using stories the children have written themselves, or stories they have heard read aloud or on tape. Folk tales are another valuable resource. Very often they exist in a similar form in the children's own culture and the repetition of language and events make it easy to predict what lies ahead.

Various preliminary activities will help prepare children for reading. For instance, you can:

- read a story aloud and invite children to supply the missing word(s) or predict what comes next

- ask children to retell a story they know, possibly using picture prompts to help them remember key incidents
- ask children to act out the story.

With more experienced children, you can read the first few paragraphs or pages yourself to key them in to the content and style of the material, or ask them to locate a key sentence in the early part of a story which gives a clue to what the story is about.

Listening to children reading

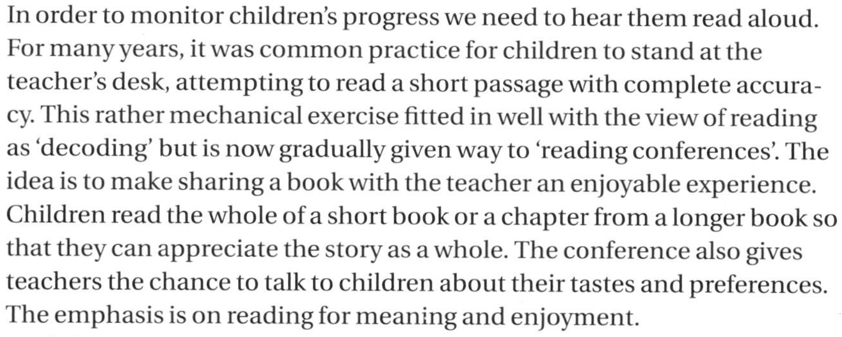

In order to monitor children's progress we need to hear them read aloud. For many years, it was common practice for children to stand at the teacher's desk, attempting to read a short passage with complete accuracy. This rather mechanical exercise fitted in well with the view of reading as 'decoding' but is now gradually given way to 'reading conferences'. The idea is to make sharing a book with the teacher an enjoyable experience. Children read the whole of a short book or a chapter from a longer book so that they can appreciate the story as a whole. The conference also gives teachers the chance to talk to children about their tastes and preferences. The emphasis is on reading for meaning and enjoyment.

It is important to remember, though, that the ultimate aim is to help them become independent readers as quickly as possible. Any teacher intervention should therefore be designed to increase their effectiveness in silent reading. It is very important, for instance, to ignore miscues which don't change the meaning. When you correct all departures from the text, the message you give is that reading is about accuracy rather then meaning. If a child reads *mummy* when the text says *mother*, the miscue doesn't change the meaning and you should not intervene.

Teachers often feel concerned when bilingual readers mispronounce a word and wonder if they should correct them. The simple answer is no. Some sounds are acquired more easily than others and there is no point in insisting on *shell* instead of *sell* if children cannot hear the difference. The same is true of inflectional endings. It is important to remember that children may say *walk* for *walked* or *jump* for *jumped* because these combinations of sounds are difficult to pronounce, not because they have failed to understand that the text is referring to something that happened in the past. Interventions of this kind are unnecessary and disturb the flow.

When children don't recognize a word, teachers can use one of several strategies, depending on the situation and the child:

- encourage children to pick up clues from illustrations
- ask a question to remind them of the context
- get them to reread the sentence with expression up to the unknown word to remind them of the context
- ask them to read to the end of the sentence and then come back to the unknown word
- give them enough time to work the word out for themselves
- say or point to the first letter of the word
- cover part of the word to make it easier to recognize
- tell the child the word to avoid losing momentum.

Non-narrative writing

It is very important for children to recognize the function of a text. We find our way round a novel or a phone book or a newspaper in different ways. We have expectations about how the text will be set out which help us to predict what comes next.

The language demands of different genres are also quite distinct (see, for instance, Perera 1984). The chronological nature of narrative makes it much closer to the ordering of speech than, for instance, information texts.

Reading to learn

Non-fiction makes much heavier demands on inexperienced readers than fiction. One obvious area of difference is vocabulary. A sentence from a science text book such as:

> The heart lies in the centre of the chest cavity

can pose a number of problems. Children may not, for instance, recognize *cavity;* and, although they may be familiar with *lies,* its use in this context may be unfamiliar.

Sentence structure is another area of difference. Non-fiction contains many passive constructions (eg *The water was placed in a beaker*) which are rarely used in speech. It also uses sentences with long phrases or subordinate clauses which make great demands on the reader's short-term memory:

> Because of a deliberate policy of divide and rule, slaves from all over Africa, speaking many different languages, were placed together.

Nominalization – where meaning is transferred from the verb to the noun – is yet another feature of non-fiction. In speech and narrative writing we might find:

> More and more people *are eating* snails.

In non-fiction, readers might encounter:

> *The eating* of snails is becoming more common.

DARTs activities

It is important to draw children's attention to these features if they are to understand what they are reading and, in due course, reproduce them in their own writing. It is also important to develop more general strategies for reading to learn. Many children deal with non-fiction by simply copying chunks of text verbatim from their books. This is a purely passive exercise: when questioned on their reading, it often becomes apparent that they have retained very little.

Children need to take a more active role: only by locating, organising and reconstructing can they make the information their own. DARTS (Directed Activities Related to Text) were developed by Lunzer & Gardner (1979; 1984) to help children interact with information texts in this way. They should grow out of topic work and not be used as isolated exercises. The usual pattern is to start with whole class discussion and then move to small group work. Finally each group reports back to the rest of the class.

Activities include:

- *Sequencing* Photocopied text is cut into sections for pairs or groups of children to reassemble and justify the order they choose.
- *Cloze procedure* Words are deleted at regular intervals in a text. Alternatively selected content words can be deleted. Children are asked to supply the missing words and justify their decision. This encourages them to use their prior knowledge and also shows them that there is usually more than one right answer.

In this example of Cloze procedure the deletion lines are of the same length. It is possible to simplify this activity by making the length of the line correspond to the deleted word, providing the first letter of the word, or giving a list of all the missing words.

```
Mammals are animals covered in fur or
........ Examples include cats, monkeys,rats
and ....... Birds (eg sparrows, finches) are
covered with ........ Reptiles (eg crocodiles
and lizards) have ........ but no fins. And
amphibians like ........ and toads have a
smooth, moist ........ covering.
```

- *Modelling* Children underline the main points in a piece of writing and present these points in the form of a chart or diagram. They can then put the information to use in a range of new ways, such as designing a poster or writing a newspaper report.

Activities of this kind offer invaluable support for the learning of *all* children, not least speakers of English as a second language who may be even less familiar than native speakers with the structures and vocabulary of information texts.

The conventions of information books

Children also need explicit teaching in 'navigating' non-fiction texts. They need to understand, for instance, the use of conventions such as headings and sub-headings, running heads, captions and the relationship of illustrations to the text, as well as the use of tools such as the contents page, index and glossary.

Bilingual support

For many years, teachers believed that the most effective form of language teaching was the direct method, where only the target language was allowed in the classroom. Today the emphasis is very different. On a theoretical level, we have a much clearer understanding of the importance of a sound foundation in the first language; on a practical level, it is a great deal more efficient to explain, where possible, key concepts and vocabulary in the first language.

Bilingual teachers can offer invaluable support for children's reading development. By asking general questions in the children's language, they can find out if children have understood what they are reading and establish the exact meaning of any unknown word.They can also encourage inference and help children to 'read between the lines'.

Paired reading

Even when there is no bilingual teacher, it is possible to enlist the help of other bilinguals – parents, grandparents, older siblings and even peers. An initiative in a London secondary school described by Jim Lamey (1989) is a case in point. Ninety-five per cent of the children in his class of 12–13 year olds were Bangladeshi. They varied a great deal in fluency in English: some were relative beginners; others had reached a high level of competence. The aim was to make the children teachers of reading and, where possible, to encourage them to work in two languages.

The first step was to stage a class discussion on the importance of reading in English and Bengali. Children's ideas were written on the board in English and translated by a fluent bilingual student. The class was then divided into groups of four and five to discuss how they could help each other improve their reading. Ideas were pooled and developed into guidelines which were translated, made into a wall chart and copied into children's Paired Reading folders.

1) I should give my partner the chance to say the word again and get it right.
2) I should only correct my partner if what he has said changes the meaning of the sentence as it appears in the book.
3) I should only give my partner a word if I am certain that he doesn't know it.
4) I should talk to my partner in English/Bengali and ask him questions to try and get him to guess the word he has got wrong.
5) I should help my partner by pointing to pictures in the story.
6) I should help my partner to understand the story by acting it out.
7) I should praise my partner when he gets something right.

The usefulness of the scheme is demonstrated from the extracts reproduced below. Shalim is a beginner in English, but a fluent reader in Bengali. He makes use of predominantly phonic skills and often has little understanding of what he reads. Enamul's English is more advanced. He, too, can read in Bengali, but not as well as Shalim. In their paired reading session, Shalim encounters: *They wished each other good day.*

Shalim: They washed each other a good day
Enamul: (in Sylheti) No. If you don't have enough money ... what do you do?
Shalim: (in Sylheti) You wish for some
Enamul: What is this in English?
Shalim: Wish
Enamul: (in Sylheti) Try the sentence again
Shalim: They wished each other a good day.

Enamul uses Sylheti to elicit a response which no picture or role play could have illustrated. He makes use of Sylheti in an equally supportive way to establish whether Shalim has understood *pleasant* in the following example:

Shalim: He hummed a pleasant tune
Enamul: (in Sylheti) What does pleasant (said in English) mean?
Shalim: (in Sylheti) Very noisy
Enamul: (in Sylheti) No. Pleasant (said in English) means nice.

Enamul used Sylheti to establish whether Shalim has understood, sometimes providing a direct translation, on other occasions asking probing questions which led him to his own solution. Nor was this support a one way process since Enamul, in turn, was able to offer Shalim help in reading Bengali.

Jim Lamey's situation, where almost all the children come from the same language background, is, of course, unusual. The same principles, however, can be applied in schools where smaller numbers of children speak the same language. Paired reading can also be organized with older and younger bilingual children, bilingual parents and children, as well as bilingual teachers and children.

Resources for reading

Individuals become literate not from the formal instruction they receive but from what they read and write about and who they read and write with.

Frank Smith (1982)

Learning to read depends on many different factors. Good quality resources may not be the most important of these factors. However, they can play a significant role in helping to promote reading as a pleasurable experience.

From the 1970s onwards, the aspect of children's literature which has received most attention from teachers in multilingual classrooms has been the importance of books which, on the one hand, are free from racial stereotypes and, on the other, reflect the cultural diversity of society. While this is an issue which concerns all children, it is particularly important that children from minority backgrounds should see themselves reflected positively in the pages of the books they read.

There has been considerable progress in the last twenty years, with the emergence of a new generation of Black and Asian writers and illustrators (Stones 1994). But, although the number of books with strong African Caribbean figures has greatly increased, South Asian and Chinese characters are still relatively rare. Books which present a positive image of ethnic minority characters can, however, can be supplemented with 'culturally neutral' materials such as traditional folk tales and stories about animals.

While concerns about cultural content remain paramount, other issues also need to be considered in choosing resources for bilingual readers. Second language learners need books with a high level of visual support which will help them to cue into what the text is all about. Equally important, they need books with a strong element of repetition and rhyme to help them predict what comes next and to internalize the rhythms, sounds and structures of English.

Older bilingual readers have additional needs. They will understandably resist books which are too babyish, either in subject matter or in the kind of illustrations they use.

Making good choices

Certain kinds of book are well suited to the needs of all emergent readers, and are particularly helpful for second language learners.

Caption books

Although caption – or concept – books have tended to go in and out of fashion over the years, there is now a general consensus that naming things is an important step in helping us make sense of the world. They are certainly helpful for bilingual readers in the early stages: as children move into their new language, there is an urgent need to learn labels for both familiar and new experiences.The strong pictorial support which caption books offer is very useful in extending children's vocabulary.

The labels used in caption books are often nouns, though sometimes they are adjectives and verbs. Very often, the illustrations are very babyish and therefore unsuitable for older readers. However, there are many notable exceptions. The *Longman Photo Dictionary* (Rosenthal & Freeman 1988) labels photos of items that will be of interest to most teenagers, including VCR, tape deck and clock radio under the heading of 'Electronics'. *ABC I can be* by Verna Wilkins (Tamarind 1993) is an alphabet book about people's jobs which suggests that anything is possible, regardless of gender or race. *Help!* (Walker 1985) and other books in the *Red nose readers* series by Allan Ahlberg will also appeal to a wide age range. Colin McNaughton's amusing illustrations combine with labels, speech bubbles and simple phrases to convey, jokes, ideas and uncomplicated stories.

Another solution to the problem of the very young 'feel' to many caption books is to use them as the starting point for children's own bookmaking activities.

Wordless picture books

Wordless picture books have emerged in recent years as an important genre in children's literature across a wide age range. They allow beginners to tell the story as they see it, and to develop an understanding of basic features such as sequence and climax.

Wordless picture books vary greatly in both style and level of complexity. Eric Carle's *Do you want to be my friend* (Puffin 1987), for instance, is a very simple story about a mouse who encounters a variety of animals while searching for a friend. The identity of each animal is hinted at by a visual cue on the preceding page.

However, many wordless texts require a high level of visual literacy which makes them particularly appropriate for older readers. Philippe Dupasquier's *The Great Escape* (Walker 1984), for instance, is an action-packed pursuit story in the style of the Keystone Cops films, full of visual jokes which will appeal to a wide age-group.

At their simplest, wordless picture books provide an opportunity to demonstrate how to use a book and left-right orientation. The pictures can be used to introduce new words or explain culture specific references. They are ideal for 'reading' in any language. Secure in the knowledge that their version is as valid as any written text, children can use the books independently, share the telling, or 'read' in English or their first language.

Page from *The Snowman* by Raymond Briggs, Puffin 1980

Samina and *The Snowman*

Angela Henry and Mike Hill (1991) tell how nine year old Samina's progress in learning English was supported by oral retellings of *The Snowman* (Briggs 1980). This is a story which, at first sight, might seem to have little cultural relevance for a child from rural Pakistan. However, it clearly caught her imagination, no doubt because of the familiar resonances with her own isolation in school and the need for friends to help her through the experience. In the early stages other bilingual pupils helped her with the oral retelling in Panjabi. Later she followed the book as she listened to another child's oral retelling of the story in English. Gradually she was able to tell the story in English on her own.

Repetition, rhythm and rhyme

In the early stages, the teacher takes the lead while children look and listen. Together, you can look at the illustrations and talk about what is happening. To begin with children often pay little or no attention to the printed words, but, by running a finger along the line, you can encourage them to look at the print .

As children's experience with books grows, they often start to join in with phrases they remember. Stories which have a strong element of repetition, rhythm and rhyme help children to predict what is coming next and to develop phonological awareness. The teacher can read up to the repetition or rhyme, then pause to let the children take over.

Good examples of books which combine repetition with strong visual support include Rebecca and Brian Wildsmith's *Look closer* (OUP 1993) which invites the reader to search for something hidden in the picture and gives the answer on the following page. Many simple retellings of traditional fairy tales work in a similar way. Jan Omerod's *The story of Chicken Licken* (Walker 1988) is particularly impressive. The story is told in picture book format by a group of children performing the play on stage. At the same time a wordless story is in progress as a baby in the audience makes a break from his parents and crawls up onto the stage.

Books such as Quentin Blake's *All join in* (Red Fox 1990) or Michael Rosen's *Freckly feet and itchy knees* (Harper Collins 1992) use rhyme as well as repetition to help children predict what comes next and carry them along with the natural rhythms of the language.

Non-fiction

Although most children are fascinated by facts, there are relatively few simply written information books. Notable exceptions include the Watts' *Ways to ...* series and the A&C Black *Messages* series. The photographic approach of these and many other series means that they are often suitable for a wide age range. However, even the simpler texts are beyond the reach of children in the early stages of learning English. Probably the best way to use materials of this kind is as the basis for discussion with the teacher.

Moving on

As children grow in independence, they begin to read the actual words, or to use the illustrations and their experience to guess what the words say. Many children enjoy reading and rereading their favourite books at this stage: their growing ability to correctly match the story to the printed text gives them a sense of security.

When choosing books for newly independent readers, several things need to be borne in mind:

- *A range of reading* Children should be exposed as early as possible to a wide range of books. Do they have opportunities for reading both fiction and non-fiction? Do they have experience of folk tales and poetry? Are there dual language books in the classroom?
- *Illustrations that support the text* There is still an urgent need for visual support. When children don't know a word, the illustrations are very powerful cues for helping them guess what it may be. Some illustrators

are much better than others at providing a close match between the illustration and the text.

- *Repetition, rhythm and rhyme* Books with predictable texts, too, are very important for both emergent and newly independent readers.
- *Familiar experiences* Bilingual readers will find it easier to predict when they are dealing with situations and concepts which are already in their experience. Of course, this doesn't mean that you can never use books which deal with things that may be unfamiliar. But before you start reading, it is important to identify and explain elements which may be new to children.
- *Stamina* Even when children's ability to make meaning from print is growing by leaps and bounds, the level of concentration required may mean that they can only sustain their reading for short stretches of time. It is important to match the length of the text to children's reading stamina. This can be done by choosing junior 'novels' divided into short chapters, or books with a strong visual element on every page.

Reading schemes

Teachers in multilingual classrooms often feel the need for a structured approach to reading for second language learners and try to identify suitable publishers' packages.

Many older reading schemes have stilted language and purposeless text, the very features which make reading so difficult. There have, however, been marked improvements in recent years. Materials published since 1990 are likely to offer a breadth of reading experience and to encourage the development of a wide range of reading strategies. They are also more likely to present positive and realistic views of gender, race and disability and to provide a richer language experience.

All the same, it is simply not possible for all children's reading requirements to be satisfied by any one editorial team, and packages will always need to be supplemented with other materials. It is also important to be aware of the competitive element associated with packaged materials, as children race to finish the scheme. For those making rapid progress, this is not a problem; but for those experiencing difficulty, the need to make their way through a rigidly ordered package of books will simply reinforce a sense of failure and frustration.

EFL series

Series especially written for the English as a Foreign Language market also look, at first sight, as though they might provide a supportive framework for learning. In actual fact, many of the criticisms of the older reading schemes apply here, too. Books are graded according to the complexity of vocabulary, sentence length or both. The language is often unnatural and the cultural content totally inappropriate. Reading materials of this kind are often more difficult for second language learners.

Multilingual resources

Books in other languages have been a feature of many schools for some time. They first appeared in the late 1970s when teachers were starting to see linguistic diversity as a resource rather than a problem. The earliest arrivals were imported books, particularly from India, in languages such as Bengali, Gujarati, Panjabi and Urdu. Most of these books were, of course, destined for the rapidly burgeoning networks of community schools.

Dual language books

The advent of dual language texts was another important landmark. Books in English and a range of other languages were seized upon as something very exciting by monolingual teachers. Bilingual teachers, however, often felt more cautious. They were better placed to judge features such as the quality of translation. They were also concerned that, as long as there was an English text, bilingual children would have little motivation to read the other language. Then there were the status issues: because of difficulties around non-latin scripts, the second language was all too often handwritten, looking very much the poor relation next to the typeset English text. Which language should come first? And so on.

There are also questions around how books are used. Is it enough simply to place them in the classroom, or does the teacher need to develop strategies for promoting them with children? And how do children use the books? The findings of the Multilingual Resources for Children Project (1995) suggest that dual language books are read in several different ways, eg English text first, then the other language; the other language first, cross-referencing to the English when they come across a word or phrase they don't recognize.

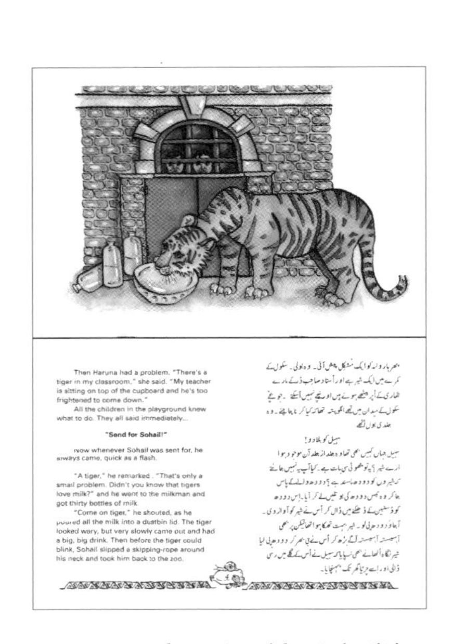

Then Haruna had a problem. "There's a tiger in my classroom," she said. "My teacher is sitting on top of the cupboard and he's too frightened to come down."

All the children in the playground knew what to do. They all said immediately...

"Send for Sohail!"

Now whenever Sohail was sent for, he always came, quick as a flash.

"A tiger," he remarked . "That's only a small problem. Didn't you know that tigers love milk?" and he went to the milkman and got thirty bottles of milk.

"Come on tiger," he shouted, as he poured all the milk into a dustbin lid. The tiger looked wary, but very slowly came out and had a big, big drink. Then before the tiger could blink, Sohail slipped a skipping-rope around his neck and took him back to the zoo.

An opening from *Send for Sohail!* by Grange Road First School, Bradford. Partnership Publishing 1993

Even though dual language books pose problems for both publishers and readers, we mustn't lose sight of the important role which they can play in classrooms. Given a little imagination and forethought on the part of teachers, these books have the potential to raise the status of other languages in general. They also offer opportunities for bilingual children to demonstrate their skills, and for monolingual children to extend their knowledge about language.

The educational reforms of recent years have tended to focus teachers' attention in other directions and linguistic diversity has taken a back seat. The number of new titles is disappointingly low, as small community publishers are left increasingly to carry the mantle. Because it is a more economic proposition to buy the rights for an existing book than to commission a new title, most recent publications are adaptations of good quality picture books such as Mary Hoffman's *Amazing Grace* (Magi 1994) or Martin Waddell's *Farmer Duck* (Magi 1993).

Important exceptions to this general trend include two titles from Partnership Publishing which make a design feature of the use of two languages, giving equal value to texts read in opposite directions. The first, *Send for Sohail!* was written by a group of children and illustrated by an artist who worked with them in their school. On each double-page spread, a full-colour illustration is set above two columns of text: English on the left, Urdu on the right. This book combines the popular super-hero theme with a simple repetitive text, making it an ideal picture book for the primary age range.

The moving mango tree and other tales by Zohra Jabeen contains two separate books within the same cover, the English version on the left hand side and the Urdu on the right. Meticulously detailed illustrations appear at the appropriate place on one of the four pages visible at any one time.

THE BAD CROW

Crows are everywhere as you know. They may have their nests in the jungle but they are always found in and around the towns and cities. And if you live in the town you can see hundreds and hundreds of crows flying back to the jungle in the evening.

One day when a big lorry was unloading salt in the market a huge piece fell down and rolled away into a corner where nobody noticed it. A clever crow was looking at it from a roof top. He flew down and dragged the piece to a safe place behind a wall. Later, when the market place was quiet, he lifted the great piece of salt onto his back, and, with some struggling, he took it to his nest.

"What should I do with it?" The crow began to wonder as soon as he had got his breath back. He gave it some thought and had the idea of building a house with the salt. Now this took some time but at last he built it. It was a dream house, snow-white, glassy and beautiful. Living in such a place a black crow should naturally feel proud and especially so did this fellow. He cut himself off from the other birds thinking he was now much too important to be seen with them.

Now it rained heavily one day and drowned the crow's salt house. The crow felt very sad and beaten sitting on just a bare branch. For quite some time he flew between the homes of the ordinary birds to take shelter. But everyone turned their backs on him and no one let him in. At last he knocked at the door of little sparrow.

"Please let me in, dear sister" he requested. The little sparrow looked doubtful knowing of his selfish ways.

"Only for a while, sister," he said, "Until I am able to find a place of my own."

A four page spread from *The moving mango tree* and other tales by Zohra Jabeen. Partnership Publishing 1992

Teacher-produced materials

Many teachers work with parents and children to 'publish' multilingual resources – both single language and dual language books – for use within the school. Some community language support services produce learning resources for local or even national distribution (Multilingual resources for Children Project 1995). Details of these publications can be obtained from the AIMER database (see Useful addresses, page 28).

Assessing reading

Traditionally, reading was assessed using standardized tests. This approach has been widely criticized: standardized tests provide little information about the reading strategies that children use or whether they can apply these strategies in new situations; they yield scores which are often difficult to interpret and give no useful indications as to how children can move forward; and they are linguistically and culturally biased in favour of White middle class children.

New understandings of literacy and learning have led to more wide ranging methods of assessment designed to help teachers make informed decisions about supporting children's development as readers.

Reading as a developmental process

Standardized tests are norm-referenced: children's performance is measured in relation to other children. More recently, there has been a move towards criterion-referenced assessment which looks at whether children can do a specific task or range of tasks. It is possible, for instance, to describe various different stages as children make their way towards becoming fully independent readers (see, for instance, Barrs *et al*,1988) and Moon & Raban, 1992):

- *Beginner readers* rely on another person to read aloud and may not be aware that text carries meaning.
- *Non-fluent readers* begin to show an interest in the printed text. They track from the top to bottom of the page and left to right, one page after another. They use illustrations and the print itself to check their predictions.
- *Moderately fluent readers* start predicting sentence ends and show an awareness of one to one word-voice match. They begin to identify initial letters of words and use these, together with pictures, to interpret meaning.
- *Fluent readers* cope well with familiar texts, monitoring meaning and self-correcting, using context and grapho-phonic cues. However, they still read word by word and their decoding is often inaccurate.
- *Exceptionally fluent readers* are able to both read known words and to decode unknown words. They scan ahead and monitor punctuation, using all available cue systems.

A holistic approach to assessment

The emphasis on reading for meaning has led teachers to assess children's development as readers in much broader terms. What do they read? What are their tastes and preferences? How successful are they at retrieving information from books? How well do they understand what they are reading? Observation is one useful assessment tool; periodic questioning in 'reading conferences' is another.

Teachers can keep records in a variety of forms: by making notes on index cards; by ticking checklists; or by writing comments on record sheets such as those provided in *The Primary Language Record* (Barrs *et al* 1988) or in *Record keeping and assessment in English* (Karavis 1995). Children can also be involved in this process by keeping reading logs or reading diaries.

It is more difficult for monolingual teachers to accurately assess bilingual children than their monolingual peers.Teachers may assume, for instance, that children's experiences are limited on the basis of what they can say in English. However, by asking parents or getting a bilingual adult to talk to the children in question, it is often possible to build up a much clearer picture of their actual experience and abilities.

Entries in a diary of observations

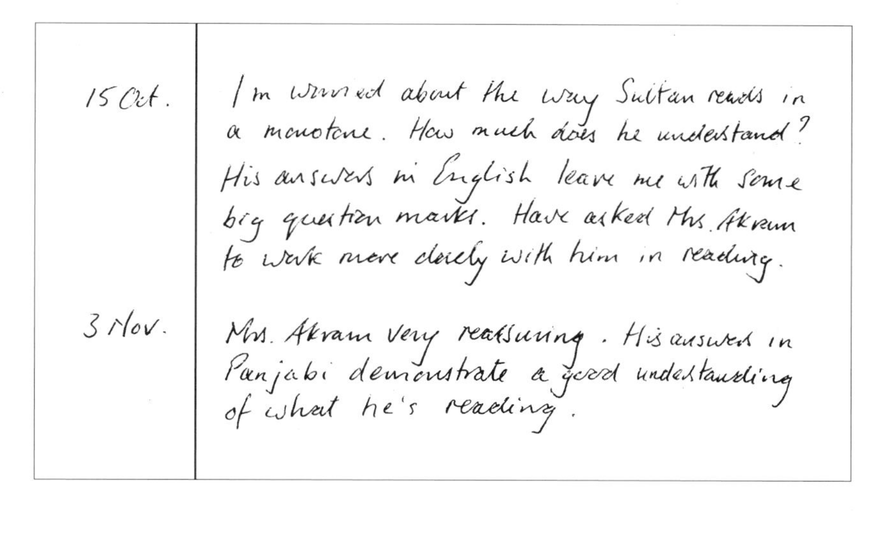

15 Oct.	I'm worried about the way Sultan reads in a monotone. How much does he understand? His answers in English leave me with some big question marks. Have asked Mrs. Akram to work more closely with him in reading.
3 Nov.	Mrs. Akram very reassuring. His answers in Panjabi demonstrate a good understanding of what he's reading.

Assessing reading strategies

Fluent readers use a wide range of strategies; less experienced readers will be more limited. Analysis of the kinds of strategies that children are currently using can therefore help to build a picture of areas where they need more help.

In the very early stages, observation is the best method of assessment. Children exposed to print for the first time – whether they are very young English speakers or Bangladeshi teenagers with no experience of literacy in English – make their way through the same developmental stages. Key questions at this point include: are they aware of the orientation of books – front-to-back, top-to-bottom, left-to-right? Do they recognise individual words and letters?

As children move towards independence, reading the words on a page – or at least saying what they think the words are – miscue analysis comes into play. Although a full miscue analysis is both long and complex, various simplified approaches can be used. The recording scheme illustrated overleaf, for instance, allows you to monitor children's cuing systems. It also helps you to focus on a number of important points: level of confidence, as indicated by the number or proportion of refusals; self-corrections that demonstrate the child is reading for meaning; and the extent to which reading fluency matches the level of difficulty of the book.

DATE 16·3·95 NAME Matthew CLASS 5 AGE 7 YEAR 2

TITLE & PAGE(S) OF BOOK Goldilocks and the Three Bears

	SUBSTITUTIONS		Similarity			
	Word printed	Word read	Sound	Look	Part of speech	Meaning
1	LITTLE	~~SMALL~~				
2	TINY	SMALL	✗	✗	✓	✓
3	WELL	BUT	✗	✗	✓	✓
4	NEVER	NOT	✓	✗	✓	✓
5						
6						
7						
8						
9						
10						
11						
12						

Tally of refusals	~~||||~~ |

Negative miscue rate $= \dfrac{\text{Meaning (X) PLUS Refusals}}{\text{Total no. of words read}} \times 100 = \dfrac{6}{178} \times 100$

$=$ 3 4 %

LEVEL = independent/instructional/frustration
(1%) ↑ (5%) (10%)

Notes on Miscue Analysis Readability of book about right; encourage him to attempt words. Some consonant work?

Record sheet from *Assessing reading strategies at key stage 1* by Cliff Moon, Reading and Language Information Centre 1990

References

Barrs, M., Ellis, S., Hester, H. & Thomas, A. (1988) *The primary language record.* London: Centre for Language in Primary Education.

Canadian Ethnocultural Council (1988) *The other Canadian languages: a report on the status of heritage languages across Canada.* Ottowa: Canadian Ethnocultural Council.

Gregory, E. (1993a) Reading between the lines. *Times Educational Supplement* 15 October: 4.

Gregory E. (1993b) Sweet and sour: learning to read in a British and Chinese school. *English in Education* 27(3): 53–9.

Heath, S.B. (1983) *Ways with words: language, life and work in communities and classrooms.* Cambridge: Cambridge University Press.

Henry, A. & Hill, M. (1991) Powerful stories. Case Study 3.18. In Open University (1991) *Talk and learning 5–16: an in-service pack on oracy for teachers.* Milton Keynes: Open University Press, pp A205–9.

Horvath, B. & Vaughan, P. (1991) *Community languages: a handbook.* Clevedon, Avon: Multilingual Matters.

Karavis, S. (1995) *Record keeping and assessment in English.* Reading: Reading and Language Information Centre, University of Reading.

Kenway, P. (1994) *Working with parents.* Reading: Reading and Language Information Centre, University of Reading.

Lamey, J. (1989) The power of partners: reading and bilingual learners. *The English Magazine* 22: 24–8.

Linguistic Minorities Project (1985) *The other languages of England.* London: Routledge.

Lunzer, E. & Gardner, K. (1979) *The effective use of reading.* London: Heinemann.

Lunzer & Gardner (1984) *Learning from the written word.* Edinburgh: Oliver & Boyd.

Minns, H. (1990) *Read with me.* London: Virago.

Moon, C. (1990) *Assessing reading strategies at key stage 1.* Reading: Reading and Language Information Centre, University of Reading.

Moon, C. & Raban, B. (1992) *A question of reading* (2nd edn). London: David Fulton.

Multilingual Resources for Children Project (1995) *Building bridges: multilingual resources for children.* Clevedon, Avon: Multilingual Matters.

Perera, K. (1984) *Children's writing and reading: analyzing classroom language.* Oxford: Blackwell.

Smith, F. (1982) *Writing and the writer.* London: Heinemann.

Street, B. (1984) *Literacy in theory and practice.* Cambridge: Cambridge University Press.

Stones, R. (ed.) (1994) *A multicultural guide to children's books 0–12.* Reading: Reading and Language Information Centre, University of Reading with Books for Keeps.

Tizard, J., Schofield, W. & Hewison, J. (1982) Symposium: reading collaboration between teachers and parents in assisting children's reading. *British Journal of Educational Psychology* 52: 1–15.

Wallace, C. (1985) *Learning to read in a multicultural society: the social context of second language literacy.* Oxford: Pergamon.

Useful addresses

AIMER (Access to Information on Mutlicultural Education Resources)
Reading and Language Information Centre
University of Reading
Bulmershe Court
Earley
Reading RG6 1HY
(tel 01734 875123 ext 4871)

Publishes annually updated lists of teaching resources in all areas of the curriculum and for language support and community language teaching.

Magi Publications
112 Whitfield Street,
London W1P 5RU
(tel 0171 387 0610)

Publishes dual language books in a range of languages.

Mantra Publishing
5 Alexandra Grove
London N12 8NU
(tel 0181 445 5123)

Publishes dual language books in a range of languages.

Partnership Publishing
Bradford & Ilkley Community College
Department of Teaching Studies
Bradford
West Yorkshire BD7 1AY

Publishes dual language books in Urdu and English.

Roy Yates Books
Smallfield Cottage
Cox Green
Rudgwick
Horsham
West Sussex RH12 3DE
(tel 01403 822299)

Lists and supplies every known dual language book in print in the UK and other English speaking countries, along with many other multilingual resources from all over the world.